Abigail Adams:

First Lady of the United States
A Short Biography

By Doug West, Ph.D.
C&D Publications

Abigail Adams: First Lady of the United States
A Short Biography
By Doug West, Ph.D.

Copyright © 2021 Doug West
All Rights Reserved. No part of this book may be reproduced or stored in a retrieval system, or transmitted in any form or by any means, electronic, mechanical, photocopying, recording or otherwise without written permission from the publisher.
Reviewers may quote brief passages in reviews.

ISBN: 9798787844788

Table of Contents

Preface 1

Introduction 3

Chapter 1 - Early Years 6

Chapter 2 - The American Revolution........................... 11

Chapter 3 – Europe 18

Chapter 4 – A Political Life in America...................... 23

Chapter 5 - The First Lady of the United States........... 28

Chapter 6 - The Children of John and Abigail Adams . 34

Chapter 7 - Retirement and Final Years 40

Timeline of the Life and Times of Abigail Adams....... 45

Biographical Sketches 47

Note of Quotes... 52

References and Further Reading.................................. 53

Acknowledgements 55

About the Author.. 56

Additional Books in the 30 Minute Book Series 57

Index 61

Preface

Welcome to the book, *Abigail Adams: First Lady of the United States: A Short Biography*. This book is volume 58 of the 30 Minute Book Series, and as the name of the series implies, if you are an average reader this book should take less than an hour to read. Since this short book is not meant to be an all-encompassing biography of Abigail Adams, you may want to know more about her life and times. To help you with this, there are several good references at the end of this book. I have also provided a Timeline, in order to link together the important events in her life, and a section of the book titled "Biographical Sketches," which includes brief biographies of some of the key individuals in the book. In the text, those individuals who are in one of the biographical sketches will have their name in **bold** print the first time they appear in the book.

Thank you for purchasing this book. I hope you enjoy your time reading about the second First Lady of the United States.

Doug West
December 2021

DOUG WEST, PH.D.

Introduction

The letter came in October of 1779 from the Congress in Philadelphia: John had been chosen virtually unanimously to represent the newly formed United States in France to negotiate a treaty of peace and commerce with Great Britain. Both John and his wife Abigail knew the perils of a winter crossing of the Atlantic—the seas were rough, and the storms were fierce. To add to her fears of his new assignment an ocean away, John was a man marked for death by the British as a traitor. She knew if his ship were captured on the high seas by a British man-of-war, he would die a traitor's death. The war for independence of the 13 colonies from Great Britain would impose a great cost on John and Abigail Adams.

Joining him on the trip were their two sons, John Quincy, age twelve, and Charles, age nine. Shortly after her husband and her two dear sons had set sail, Abigail put to paper the feelings of her uneasy spirit in a letter to John: "My hopes and fears rise alternately. I cannot resign more than I do, unless life itself was called for.— My dear sons I cannot think of them without a tear, little do they know the feelings of a Mothers Heart!" She knew it would be months before he received the letter, but she had to put words on paper.

John Quincy had already been to France once on his father's first diplomatic mission and wanted to stay at home with his mother to continue his schooling. But Abigail insisted he go, telling the boy of the great opportunity that lay before him. After the men in her life had been gone for two months, in the cold of a New England winter, Abigail wrote these words of encouragement to her eldest son: "These are times in which a Genius would wish to live. It is not in the still calm of life, or the repose of a pacific station, that great characters are formed." Even though she knew of the great peril he would face, she encouraged the boy to think beyond this time of distress and realize this trial would forge him into a great man. "The Habits of a vigorous mind are formed in contending with difficulties" Abigail wrote. "All History will convince you of this, and that wisdom and penetration are the fruits of experience, not the Lessons of retirement and leisure." John Quincy must have taken some of her words to heart, as in the years to come he would follow in his father's footsteps to become the president of the United States.

It would be four years before Abigail would reunite with John and John Quincy, though Charles returned home after two years in Europe. This long separation was hard on all of them; John and the two boys were in a foreign country, and she was at home tending to the farm and young children in a war-torn land. The War for Independence had brought havoc to the colony's economy, food and necessities were scarce, their paper money had been reduced to pennies on the dollar due to the rampant inflation, and the war persisted like a dry winter cough that would not relent.

This was just one of the trials this amazing woman would face over the course of her life. As her husband ascended the ranks of the new government of the United States, finally achieving the presidency, Abigail remained steadfast at his side. She offered not only the comfort a spouse can bring, but insights into the inner workings of the political theater in which John was engrossed. She was his intellectual equal, which is saying a lot since John Adams has been ranked as one of the brightest presidents who ever served.

This is the story of a feisty New England wife and mother who helped forge the destiny of a new nation.

Chapter 1 - Early Years

"My bursting heart must find vent at my pen."
– Abigail Adams

Abigail Smith was the daughter of a Congregationalist minister, William Smith, and his wife Elizabeth Quincy Smith. Abigail was born on November 22, 1744, in her parents' house in Weymouth, Massachusetts Bay Colony. The town of Weymouth, just fourteen miles from Boston, was one of the towns that dotted the New England coastline. Abigail grew up with the sights and sounds of the sea filling her days. Her family was well respected in the Massachusetts Bay Colony and active in politics. True to her Puritan roots, she was brought up in a stern and structured household. Since formal schooling was not the norm for young girls in colonial New England and her health was frail, she was educated at home by her parents. Using the books in her father's, uncle's, and grandfather's libraries, Abigail and her sisters read widely in English and French literature.

Though her education was meager, she loved to read and became one of the best-read women of her time. Abigail was also a prolific letter writer in her youth and carried this trait into adulthood. Through her letters, of which roughly 2,000 have survived, generations of Americans have been able to gain a glimpse of her personality and daily life in colonial America.

Figure - Birthplace of Abigail Adams in Weymouth, Massachusetts.

Marriage to John Adams

John Adams had known the Smith family since his youth, but he paid little attention to Reverend Smith's middle daughter. Things changed in 1762 when he tagged along with his friend Richard Cranch, who was engaged to the oldest Smith daughter, Mary. John started to take notice of the petite, shy seventeen-year-old brunette who seemed to always have her head in a book. He was surprised to learn that she knew so much about poetry, philosophy, and politics. Adams was a Harvard educated lawyer and fell for the "saucy" (his word) young woman nearly ten years his junior. John's family was not as well placed in colonial Massachusetts society as hers, leading to an initial rejection of John as a serious suitor by her mother. Her family feared his meager income as a country lawyer was not sufficient to support a wife and raise a family; also, his manners reeked of the farm. Over time as their relationship grew, her family relaxed their opposition to the courtship.

After a lengthy engagement, John and Abigail were married October 25, 1764, at the Weymouth parsonage in a small service conducted by her father. Abigail wore a square-necked gown of white challis. The groom wore a dark blue coat, contrasting light breeches, and a gold-embroidered satin waistcoat his mother had made for the occasion. As soon as the wedding ceremony was complete and the guests had all been greeted, the newlyweds rode off together on John's horse to his farm at Braintree. (The town was later renamed Quincy in honor of her family on her mother's side). At the time of her wedding, she was not quite twenty, little more than five feet tall, with dark brown hair, brown eyes, and a smooth, pale complexion. In his diary, John describes her as "prudent, soft, sensible, obliging, active." Two years later she wrote of him, "My Good Man is so very fat…"

John had inherited a small house and farm upon the death of his father, and this would be their new home. Abigail would have her hands full with John, who could sometimes be prickly, vain, and a bit erratic. In a letter a few years later, she would describe the bond between them as "a tye more binding than Humanity, and stronger than Friendship, which makes us anxious for the happiness and welfare of those to whom it binds us. It makes their Misfortunes, Sorrows, and affliction, our own."

Figure – Portrait of Abigail Adams by Benjamin Blyth, circa 1766.

Letters

John's job as a lawyer and his involvement in the resistance movement against British aggression kept him away from home much of the time. While John was away for extended periods, Abigail managed the farm and the growing family. Neither enjoyed the separations, but they were committed to the public good and viewed the long absences as a necessary evil. While they were away from each other they corresponded regularly, giving the modern reader insight into their personal lives. Unlike **Martha Washington**, who burnt all her personal letters after her husband's death, Abigail and John Adams kept many of their personal letters. They have been cataloged by historians and are available to the public online.

The letters reveal that John viewed his wife as an intellectual equal, which, again, is no small statement since John Adams is considered one of the great political thinkers of the American revolutionary era. Abigail was her husband's trusted advisor, and he often took her advice on personal and professional matters. Both were passionate about their family and shared a common hope for the future of their new nation.

The separations were hard on both of them, but Abigail once remarked that she was "the greatest sufferer." Once when she hadn't heard from her husband for five weeks, she exclaimed, "I had rather give a dollar for a letter by the post, tho the consequence should be that I Eat but one meal a day for these three weeks to come." Though John was often deeply immersed in his work he missed her too. In a letter from Amsterdam in 1781 he confessed, "What a fine Affair it would be if We could flit across the Atlantic as they say Angels do from Planet to Planet. I would dart to Penns Hill and bring you over on my Wings."

Chapter 2 - The American Revolution

"Arbitrary power is like most other things which are very hard, very liable to be broken." – Abigail Adams

Not long after John and Abigail were married, tensions between the British and the American colonists began to escalate. The colonists opposed, sometimes violently, the increased taxes levied upon the British colonies in America. John was a well-educated colonial lawyer who moved to the forefront of the movement to seek independence from England. Though the British won the French and Indian War with France, Britain was deeply in debt and looked to the prosperous colonies for tax revenue. The colonists were opposed to the British demands primarily because they had no voice in the British Parliament.

The Boston Massacre in 1770, where five colonists were killed by British troops, and the Boston Tea Party in 1773, where over 300 chests full of British tea were dumped into Boston Harbor in protest over the tax on tea, were events that came to be emblematic of the bitter struggle between the colonists and the mother country. Just two weeks before the Boston Tea Party, Abigail had written her friend, the noted author **Mercy Otis Warren**, and revealed her zeal for an action against the hated British tea: "The Tea that baneful weed is arrived.

Great and I hope Effectual opposition has been made to the landing of it...The flame is kindled and like Lightening it catches from Soul to Soul. Great will be the devastation if not timely quenched..." Abigail and Mercy visited and corresponded with each other for many years, discussing their thoughts on writers, politics, children, fashion, and their husbands.

Both John and Abigail were very aware of the developing animosity between the residents of colonial New England and the mother country. Since the Boston area was a hotbed of the resistance, John, Abigail, and their family were in the middle of the conflict. The town of Boston, with some 16,000 residents, supported several newspapers that the couple read daily. They grew more incensed with the needless aggression of the British and both believed separation from Great Britain was the only way for the colonies to grow and prosper.

John was called upon to travel to Philadelphia in 1774 to represent Massachusetts in the First Continental Congress. Though by today's standards the 300 miles between Boston and Philadelphia is just a few hours car ride, in the late eighteenth century, the journey typically took over a week. This separation of the couple would be the first of many.

The Battle of Bunker Hill

In April 1775 the war of words with the British turned to open warfare at a skirmish between the colonial militia and British regular soldiers or "red coats," as the rebels called them. The battles at Lexington and at Concord,

Massachusetts, marked the beginning of a war between Great Britain and the 13 colonies that would drag on for eight long years. With British troops already stationed at Boston, the area became the location of the first major battle of the American Revolutionary War.

In the early hours of June 17, 1775, Abigail and her children (John was still away at Congress in Philadelphia) were awakened to the sound of cannon fire to the north. At dawn, John Quincy and his mother climbed Penn's Hill to see what all the noise was about. From the top of the hill, they could see fighting in Boston about ten miles away. When the smoke cleared and the roar of the cannons ceased, hundreds of men lay dead or wounded on the field of battle. "How many have fallen we know not," she wrote to John that night. "The constant roar of the cannon is so distressing that we cannot eat, drink, or sleep." Though the victory in the battle was given to the British, the red coats learned that day that the Continental Army, made up of volunteer farmers and merchants, was a force not to be trifled with.

"Remember the Ladies" Letter

While John was away at the Second Continental Congress in Philadelphia, Abigail wrote to him on March 31, 1776, reminding him of his responsibilities to "Remember the Ladies" in the new "Code of Laws" he and the other delegates were in the process of drafting. In colonial America, married women had few rights: they couldn't vote, own property, or hold a public office. Abigail wanted her husband and the other delegates to take seriously the need for women to have rights in the new republic. In the letter she wrote, "Remember the Ladies, and be more generous and favorable to them than your ancestors. Do not put such unlimited power into the hands of the Husbands. Remember all Men would be tyrants if they could. If particular care and attention is not paid to the Ladies we are determined to foment a Rebellion, and will not hold ourselves bound by any Laws in which we have no voice, or Representation. That your Sex are Naturally Tyrannical is a Truth so thoroughly established as to admit of no dispute, but such of you as wish to be happy willingly give up the harsh title of Master for the more tender and endearing one of Friend. Why then, not put it out of the power of the vicious and the Lawless to use us with cruelty and indignity with impunity. Men of Sense in all Ages abhor those customs which treat us only as the vassals of your Sex. Regard us then as Beings placed by providence under your protection and in imitation of the Supreme Being make use of that power only for our happiness."

John's letter in response is dated April 14, 1776, which was a rather fast reply by colonial standards. In the letter he gives a lighthearted response, though not ignoring her request. He responded, "As to your extraordinary Code of Laws, I cannot but laugh. We have been told that our Struggle has loosened the bands of Government everywhere. That Children and Apprentices were disobedient—that schools and Colleges were grown turbulent—that Indians slighted their Guardians and

Negroes grew insolent to their Masters. But your Letter was the first Intimation that another Tribe more numerous and powerful than all the rest were grown discontented.—This is rather too coarse a Compliment but you are so saucy, I won't blot it out."

The letter from Abigail, which has become known in history as "Remember the Ladies," and John's response have been marked by historians as some of the earliest writings regarding the women's rights movement in America. It would take until the 20th century before women would get the same legal rights as men, explicitly in the 19th Amendment to the Constitution which gave women the right to vote in 1920. Abigail's letter clearly shows she was ahead of her time and an agent of change in colonial America.

Figure – Reverse of the 2007 U.S. Mint half ounce gold medal featuring Abigail Adams penning her "Remember the Ladies" letter to her husband.

Smallpox Epidemic

The deadly viral illness smallpox, which killed about one in three of those infected, was a constant threat to colonists and especially the Native Americans, who had no natural immunity. The disease had been brought to North America by the Spanish in the 16th century. When outbreaks occurred, which they did regularly, it struck fear in the colonists as they knew people would die. Early in the 18th century the idea of inoculation of a healthy person with a small skin sample from an infected person was becoming accepted, although very controversial. The problem was that, unlike modern vaccines that don't contain a live virus, this method of inoculation introduced the healthy person to a live smallpox virus. In most cases the inoculated person got sick but recovered, thus being rendered immune to the disease for the remainder of their life. What made this method of preventive medicine so controversial, however, was that a fair number of those inoculated died a horrible death.

Abigail feared the dreaded disease and sought the help of a Boston doctor to administer the smallpox inoculation to her family. In July 1776, just a week after the Declaration of Independence had been adopted, Abigail took her four children, other family members, and servants to Boston to stay in the large home of her uncle Isaac Smith. All were immunized and began to fall ill. Abigail wrote fearfully to John, telling him, "The Little folks are very sick and puke every morning but after that they are comfortable." All John could do was worry about his family and the men in the Continental Army as the disease swept through the ranks. He had been inoculated during the smallpox epidemic of 1764 and was therefore not concerned for his own health. John reported to Abigail with trepidation, "The Small Pox, has done Us more harm than British armies, Canadians, Indians, Negroes, Hanoverians, Hessians, and all the rest."

By July 18 Abigail was well enough to attend Boston's celebration for the Declaration of Independence; however, her children remained sick. She reported that, "Nabby has enough of the smallpox for all the family beside. She is pretty well covered, not a spot of what is so sore that she can neither walk, sit, stand, or lay with any comfort." With pustules the size of peas, Nabby was miserable. In another letter she wrote that six-year-old Charles was burning with fever and went into a delirium that lasted 48 hours. After nearly a two month stay at her uncle's house the family was able to return to Braintree.

Chapter 3 – Europe

"I am more and more convinced that man is a dangerous creature and that power, whether vested in many or a few, is ever grasping, and like the grave, cries, 'Give, give.' " – Abigail Adams

In the early years of the War of Independence the colonists fared poorly against the seasoned and well-equipped British army. The Congress, including John Adams, knew it was necessary for their infant country to have France as their ally in the struggle with Britain. In 1778, John was appointed as Commissioner to France to work with Benjamin Franklin and Author Lee to establish an alliance between the two nations. To fulfill his new role, John set sail for France; along on the voyage was his ten-year-old son John Quincy. This would begin a long period of separation between Abigail and John and their eldest son.

Even before the Declaration of Independence was signed in 1776, Abigail realized that John was consumed with the revolution and the effort to build a new nation, and she became reconciled to the fact that it meant great sacrifice for her family. She affirmed to John: "I can serve my partner, my family and myself, and enjoy the Satisfaction of your service to your country." With the departure of John to Europe she knew that the education of the children, management of the farm, and all other domestic duties would fall upon her shoulders. With an ocean separating them, their letters became a lifeline to keep their relationship alive. In that time, communication between continents was slow; a letter would take anywhere from one to three months to travel across the sea, then another similar period before a response came. To complicate matters, the British navy enforced blockades of the coast of North America, seizing ships and confiscating cargo of the ships they captured. To Abigail's relief, John returned to Massachusetts from his diplomatic work in Europe during the summer of 1779.

Diplomat to France

John's stay at home was brief as Congress called him once again to duty in France. This new assignment was tough for Abigail to take as her husband had only been home for a few short months. In November 1779, John along with their sons John Quincy and Charles departed for Europe. Since the American colonies and Great Britain were still at war, travel across the Atlantic was treacherous. Abigail feared for the safety of John and the two boys. John, Benjamin Franklin, and **Thomas Jefferson** were tasked with establishing commercial treaties and arranging loans for the United States.

In the fall of 1783, John helped negotiate a treaty of peace between the fledgling United States of America and Great Britain. After the Revolutionary War ended,

John remained in France as the new nation's minister. He encouraged Abigail to join him. After four years of separation Abigail decided to calm her fear of an ocean voyage and wrote to tell him, "The desires and request of my Friend are a Law to me. I will sacrifice my present feelings and hope for a blessing in pursuit of my duty." On June 20, 1784, Abigail, Nabby, and two servants set sail from Boston bound for Europe. Though the trip took over a month and all were subject to violent bouts of sea sickness, they arrived safely in London. There, John Quincy, now in his late teens, met his mother and sister. John joined them a week later. Once they had recovered from the rigors of the sea voyage they traveled to Paris and settled in a luxurious home on the banks of the Seine River in the Paris suburbs.

In letters home to friends and family in America, Abigail revealed a life in France that was more leisurely than she had experienced running the farm back in Massachusetts. Like her husband she disapproved of much of the fun-loving spirit and more open lifestyle of the Parisians. The other American minister in France, Thomas Jefferson, a widower, had brought his young daughter Martha to stay with him. Jefferson and the Adamses became close while they were living in France. Abigail became a mother figure to Martha, and the two became close. Jefferson took John Quincy under his wing, becoming a mentor to the brilliant young man. When the Adamses left France for John's new position in England, Abigail wrote her sister, "I shall really regret to leave Mr. Jefferson; he is one of the choice ones on earth."

England 1785

After the War for Independence, Congress appointed John as the American ambassador to the English Court of St. James with the task of healing the relationship between the two countries. John Quincy returned to America for college while John, Abigail, and Nabby moved into a lovely home on Grosvenor Square in an elegant part of London. Abigail's stay in France was less than a year, but she would spend the next three years in England.

As the wife of the American ambassador, many doors to high-ranking English men and women were opened to Abigail. She got to see firsthand how the monarchical system of government worked. Not long after they arrived in London, John, Abigail, and Nabby had an audience with King George III and his wife Charlotte. After waiting in a long line to meet the king and queen, they were introduced to the royal couple and exchanged pleasantries. Abigail reported to her sister that she found the royals rather dull and was glad that the ordeal was over. The Adamses would cross paths with the monarch at several official functions during their years in England.

Though Abigail was a bit put off with the pomp and ceremony in the British royal court, she much preferred it to the French Court of Louis XVI. In England, she could speak her native tongue, whereas in France, her command of the French language was rudimentary at best. She much preferred the American form of government, believing the English system oppressed the lower classes. In a letter to her sister, she wrote, "When I reflect upon…the millions who are loaded with taxes to support this pomp and show, I look to my happier country with an enthusiastic warmth."

In early 1787, John resigned as the United States minister to England as both he and Abigail had grown terribly homesick. It would be another year before a suitable replacement could be found for John and they could return to America. The time in France and England had greatly expanded Abigail's worldview far beyond the bucolic life of Braintree. At age 43 she was a mature woman, her youngest child was 16, and Nabby had married and given John and Abigail their first grandchild—whom Abigail adored.

Chapter 4 –
A Political Life in America

"If we do not lay out ourselves in the service of mankind whom should we serve?" – Abigail Adams

After seven long weeks at sea, the Adamses reached the shores of America and moved into a house in Braintree they had purchased sight unseen while they were in England. They named their new home "Peacefield." About the time they arrived back in America the Constitution for the United States was ratified, meaning a new form of government for the nation was established. The Constitution called for a chief executive, or president, to lead the government. The enormously popular General Washington was elected unanimously by the electoral college as the first president. As the first vice president, the electors chose John Adams by a narrow margin.

Figure – Watercolor painting of Peacefield mansion, circa 1787.

Abigail was in Massachusetts when John was sworn in as the vice president in April 1789. That summer, she joined him in New York, the seat of government for the new nation. New York was the nation's largest city with a population of some 30,000. The Adamses moved into a rented home at Richmond Hill overlooking the Hudson River, about two miles out from the city.

Abigail was keenly aware of the politics of the day and provided valuable advice and insight to her husband in his new role. Their friend Thomas Jefferson was appointed secretary of state under President Washington. It was during these early days of the Washington administration that political rivalries and differences began to surface.

As the wife of the vice president, she was quickly thrust into a whirlwind of social engagements. She wrote to her sister Mary: "Our House has been a mere Levee ever since I arrived morning & evening." Nabby and her mother went to visit First Lady Martha Washington not long after their arrival in the bustling city. Abigail was deeply impressed with Mrs. Washington's "modest, dignified, and feminine" ways. To her, Mrs. Washington exemplified female republican virtues and was a marked contrast to the haughty royalty she had been exposed to in Europe. The Washington and Adam families came to be on friendly terms, and they often visited each other socially.

The Seat of Government Moves to Philadelphia

As a result of political maneuvers and compromises, in 1790 it was decided that the seat of government would be moved to a site to be known as Washington, D.C., located on the Potomac River. In the interim period, the national government would be moved to Philadelphia. This meant for the Adamses another move. Abigail took the news in stride, writing to her sister, "Do you not pity me my dear Sister to be so soon all in a Bustle, and weary of removing again...I feel low spirited and Heartless. I am going amongst another new set of company, to form new acquaintances, to make and receive a hundred ceremonious visits not one of ten from which I shall derive a pleasure and satisfaction."

Abigail worried the change in climate from New York would affect her health. She was also fearful of Philadelphia's reputation for yellow fever outbreaks. Though she had many trepidations about the move to the new city, she was determined to make the best of the situation. As the wife of the vice president, she was required to keep up a busy social calendar, and this began to weigh on her already fragile health. However, she did find the upper-class women of Philadelphia better educated and more fluent in the politics of the day than those she had met in New York.

During much of John's second term she returned to Quincy (formally part of Braintree). John's meager salary as vice president and all the social entertaining it required had put a strain on their personal finances. This arrangement allowed John to live in a boarding house where he would not be responsible for hosting large social events. Back in Quincy, Abigail set to work restoring the family's finances and kept abreast of politics through letters with John and the newspapers. John returned to Quincy as often as his schedule allowed.

The Presidential Election of 1796

After two terms in office, President Washington refused to run for a third term, thus providing John an opportunity to fill his empty seat. The election of 1796 proved to be a close race, with Adams barely beating out Thomas Jefferson for the presidency. In the early days of the republic, the peculiar voting system required the person with the most votes to be president and the one with the second highest number of electoral votes to be vice president. The 12th amendment to the Constitution in 1804 revised the voting system to what it is today.

Just a few years before the election, political parties had formed, with Jefferson and Adams in different camps. Adams was a member of the Federalist Party, which supported a strong central government and held close ties to England. The opposition party, led by Jefferson, was the anti-Federalist or Democratic-Republican party. They favored landowners and limited power of government and were more sympathetic to the ideals of France rather than England.

Adams was the nominee for the Federalist Party, and the Democratic-Republicans chose Jefferson as their candidate. Adams won the election by a narrow margin over Jefferson. Adams took the office of the presidency with Jefferson as his vice president even though he was from the opposite political party. This antagonistic relationship hindered Adams's ability in office and turned the once cordial relationship between the two men acrimonious.

Chapter 5 -
The First Lady of the United States

"I've always felt that a person's intelligence is directly reflected by the number of conflicting points of view he can entertain simultaneously on the same topic."
– Abigail Adams

On February 8, 1797, 61-year-old John Adams was elected the second president of the United States. Abigail knew that John's role as the nation's chief executive would place a burden upon herself and her family, and she wrote: "My feelings are not that of pride, or ostentation upon the occasion. They are solemnized by a sense of the obligations, the important Trusts and Numerous Duties connected with it." John called upon his wife immediately in his new role. Though he was a brilliant man and politically astute, he needed her help to navigate the social and cultural waters surrounding the presidency.

Due to her responsibilities on their farm and the care required by her ailing mother-in-law, Abigail sent John her heartfelt congratulations but was not going to attend the March 4 inauguration. After a five-year absence from Philadelphia, in early May 1797 Abigail made the long journey to be with her husband and assume her duties as the First Lady of the United States. The first two days she spent putting her new house in order. The Adamses had rented the house that President and Mrs. Washington had lived in during their stay in the capital city. Once her house was in order, she set about defining the Adams Republican Court. Like Martha Washington who came before her and her successor Dolley Madison, Abigail clearly understood the importance of position to help her husband institute his policies.

Figure – The Presidential Mansion in Philadelphia occupied by the Adamses from 1797 to 1800.

Illness

Abigail became deathly ill in the summer of 1798 with what may have been the recurrence of malaria. She suffered from severe headaches, fever, insomnia, and rheumatism, and was diagnosed by the doctors with dysentery, a form of diabetes, and the vague term "bilious" fever. Medical science was in a sad state during the colonial period, having advanced little since the dark ages. Often the remedies prescribed by the doctors caused more harm than good. John took his wife back to Quincy and stayed with her for months. In

November she began to recover, and John was able to return to Philadelphia to resume his duties as president. Abigail remained in Massachusetts for many months before returning to Philadelphia and followed the political happenings from her home.

The Election of 1800

John Adams turned out to be an unpopular president. Gone was the aura of the presidency that George Washington had epitomized. Adams faced opposition for his determination to keep the country out of war with France and the enactment of the harsh Alien and Sedition Acts. Political power moved from the Federalists to the Republicans in the election of 1800. Adams faced his old friend turned rival Thomas Jefferson and his running mate Aaron Burr. After a contentious election that was settled in the House of Representatives, Jefferson became president with Burr his vice president—Adams was out. The election was held in December of 1800 but the determination of the new president, Jefferson or Burr, would not be finalized until February 1801.

The New Executive Mansion in Washington, D.C.

At the very end of Adams's term, while the election was being finalized, John moved into the partially complete Executive Mansion in the new capital city of Washington, D.C. On his first day at the new residence, he wrote Abigail expressing his hope for future presidents: "I pray heaven to bestow the best of blessings on this House and all that shall hereafter inhabit it. May none but honest and wise men ever rule under this roof." Over a century later, a future president, Franklin D. Roosevelt, had the statement engraved over the fireplace in the state dining room.

When Abigail arrived in November 1800, Washington was a rough frontier outpost. The city had been carved out of the marshy wilderness on the banks of the Potomac River on land that had once been owned by President Washington. Though John and Abigail would only spend a few short months at the new Executive Mansion—it was not called the White House until decades later—they would have the distinction of being the first to occupy the permanent new home of the president and his family.

Figure – Portrait of Abigail Smith Adams
by Gilbert Stuart, 1800-1815.

At the time the first family moved into the half-finished Executive Mansion, Washington had around 500 resident families and 300 or so government workers. Abigail wrote to her sister: "Not one room or chamber is finished in the whole." The lack of accommodations forced Abigail to entertain dignitaries in very modest quarters, and she used the empty East Room to hang her wash to dry. She kept every fireplace in the house going to keep the damp chill at bay. Though the house was quite primitive during her stay and the city of Washington lacked many of the amenities of the larger cities of Philadelphia or New York, she realized the importance of having an Executive Mansion and a capital city for the new nation.

Before Abigail left the capital city in December 1800, she visited her old friend Martha Washington at her estate, Mt. Vernon. She enjoyed the visit with the lady she admired and who had been a mentor to her on the office of the First Lady. Though Abigail was fond of Martha, she did not find the vast plantation of Mt. Vernon, which was worked primarily by over a hundred African slaves, appealing. Abigail had grown to hate the institution of slavery and how it was a direct contradiction to the idea of personal liberty expressed in the Declaration of Independence. She abhorred the idea that the President's House, in which she then lived, had been constructed upon the labor of black slaves.

Before Thomas Jefferson took over the office of the president, he stopped by the Executive Mansion for dinner with the Adamses. Though the relationship between the couple and Jefferson had been fractured by the political in-fighting during John's term as vice president and president, they remained outwardly civil. As a staunch Federalist, Abigail viewed Jefferson's election as a Republican as a tragic disaster that threatened the frail republic.

Chapter 6 - The Children of John and Abigail Adams

"Great necessities call out great virtues."
– Abigail Adams

During the course of their long marriage, John and Abigail Adams had six children, three daughters and three sons. Two of the daughters died in infancy and the remaining four children lived into adulthood. Their most famous son, John Quincy, went on to serve in government and become the sixth president of the United States. The other three children led more normal lives.

Abigail Amelia "Nabby" Adams (1765 – 1813)

Their first daughter, named after her mother, Abigail Amelia, was born nine months after their marriage. The family called her "Nabby" and she was Abigail's constant companion for much of her life until she married. While John was away at Congress and a diplomat to France, Nabby helped her mother look after the farm and care for her younger siblings.

While living in London she fell in love with her father's secretary Colonel William Smith. They were married in London in 1786. Colonel Smith was a veteran of the Revolutionary War and ten years older than Nabby; he proved to be a loving husband and father of their four children but a poor provider. He was involved in several get-rich-quick schemes that resulted in financial loss.

In 1810, Nabby was diagnosed with breast cancer. At the time the only effective treatment was a mastectomy. After consultation with doctors the surgery was performed at the Adamses' home. The crude surgery, with opium as the only anesthetic, was believed to be a success. John recorded in a letter to his friend Dr. Benjamin Rush, who had been consulting on the case, that the doctors all agreed "that the morbid substance is totally eradicated and nothing left but Flesh perfectly sound." Abigail was relieved at the outcome of the surgery, allowing her to focus her attention on the care of her household.

Nabby eventually regained her health and returned to her home in Lebanon, New York, with her husband and daughter the summer of 1812. Soon new tumors appeared on her other breast. By the time Nabby told her mother of the return of the cancer she felt she had only a short time to live. Abigail reported the cancer had "rapidly diffused itself through her whole frame, destroyed her constitution and rendered her a perfect cripple." Nabby asked her parents to journey the 300 miles to see her one last time at the home in New York. Regretfully Abigail had to inform her daughter that she was "too infirm" to make the long trip. Nabby knew she had to make the trip to see her parents one last time before she died. The trip from New York to Quincy for Nabby was torturous; riding in a jostling carriage all that way forced her pain-wrecked body to feel every bump and divot in the primitive roads.

In late June Nabby and her caretakers arrived in Quincy. Nabby was immediately carried off to bed. As Abigail reported, "Opium was the only palliative, the only relief she could obtain, to relieve the spasms which as she described it, cased her up in armor." At age 48, her body finally was consumed by the cancer and she died on August 15, 1813. Abigail took some degree of comfort, as she told John Quincy's sons, that her daughter was "permitted and enabled to encounter a most hazardous journey in her weak state, and allowed to see her parents & friends again and to live until [Colonel Smith] returned from Congress, when as tho all her wishes were fulfilled, she cheerfully resigned her life into the hands of her maker."

Figure – Portrait of Abigail "Nabby" Adams Smith by Mather Brown, 1785.

John Quincy Adams (1767 – 1848)

Their eldest son John Quincy was born in Braintree and like his father and maternal grandfather, he attended Harvard College. Abigail knew from an early age that her son was a scholarly young man, telling her sister that he was "so much of a bookworm and scholar that he will grow negligent of those attentions which are due to the world." Before becoming president, John Quincy served in several different positions in government. As a diplomat, he played an important role in negotiating key treaties, including the Treaty of Ghent, which ended the War of 1812. As Secretary of State under President James Monroe, he negotiated with Great Britain in 1818 over the United States' northern border with Canada; negotiated the Adams-Onís Treaty with Spain, which allowed for the annexation of Florida; and drafted the Monroe Doctrine. Historians generally agree that he was one of the greatest diplomats and secretaries of state in American history.

John Quincy was elected president in a controversial four-way contest in 1824. His term as president was ineffective as he was thwarted time and again by a hostile Congress, and his lack of patronage networks helped opponents sabotage his presidency. After his one term as president, Adams was elected to the U.S. House of Representatives from Massachusetts, serving for the last seventeen years of his life with greater acclaim than he had achieved as president. Like his parents, he became a leading opponent of slavery. Up until her death in 1818, Abigail followed his career with much enthusiasm.

Charles Adams (1770 – 1800)

Their second son, Charles, would go on to lead a troubled life, causing much misery for his parents. At age nine, he accompanied his elder brother and father to Paris and Amsterdam, where Mr. Adams was negotiating for loans to allow the 13 colonies to continue their fight for independence. After two years in Europe, he returned to Massachusetts to live with his mother and sister. At age 15 he entered Harvard College to study law. There he got into trouble but graduated in 1789. It was during these years that Abigail and John became concerned about Charles's excessive alcohol consumption. After college he moved to New York to study law under the lawyers Alexander Hamilton and John Laurance. He passed the bar examination in 1792 and became a practicing attorney in New York City.

Charles married Sally Smith, Nabby's sister-in-law, and the couple had two daughters. In his late 20s his problems with alcohol escalated. He quit his law practice and began a life of debauchery. His wife and daughters were forced to live first with Nabby and then Abigail. When John was near the end of his term as president, Abigail paid one last visit to her ailing son on her way to Philadelphia to be with her husband. She passed through New York to visit Charles. He was staying at the home of a friend, where his wife was caring for him. Once she saw his bloated body and heard his delusional rantings, she realized her son was dying, an opinion confirmed by the doctors. She sadly came to the realization that this was probably the last she would see her poor troubled boy, once the darling of his father's heart, alive.

Three weeks later on November 30, 1800, Charles, at age 30, died from complications of liver and lung disease and dropsy. Abigail wrote her sister Mary in a letter ripe with a mother's pain, "Weep with me, over the grave of a poor unhappy child who cannot now add another pang to those which have pierced my Heart for several years past..."

Thomas Boylston Adams (1772 – 1832)

Like his two older brothers and father, Thomas attended Harvard and became a lawyer. After college, instead of practicing law he served as secretary to his brother John Quincy, who had been appointed minister to the Netherlands by President Washington. After returning to America, he tried his hand at law in Philadelphia but was unsuccessful. At the urging of his parents, he returned to Quincy and set up his law practice. In 1805 he married Ann "Nancy" Harrod. Together the couple had eight children in rapid succession. Thomas, like his father, was elected to the Massachusetts legislature, but only served for a year. Then in 1811 he was the chief justice of the circuit court of common pleas for Massachusetts's southern district. When his mother died in 1818, he returned to Quincy with his family to live with his father. He gave up his career in law and politics and put his energies into managing the family's farm. Like his brother Charles, Thomas had a problem with alcohol. He died deeply in debt in 1832.

Chapter 7 - Retirement and Final Years

"If we mean to have heroes, statesmen and philosophers, we should have learned women." – Abigail Adams

John's return home from Washington, D.C., was a welcomed event. They had both longed for the days when they could enjoy a more private life out of the public eye. Abigail kept busy around Peacefield taking care of her domestic duties, including the rearing of two of Nabby's children. Like John, she voraciously read the papers, keeping a close watch on the local and national political scene. Not only was she interested in American politics, her interests also went to Europe. She once wrote to John Quincy's mother-in-law, Catherine Johnson, who lived in England, asking her for updates on the Napoleonic Wars and how the administration of President James Madison was being perceived in Europe. She admitted to Catherine, "I cannot wean myself from the subject of politics."

A letter from Mercy Warren's son came in late 1814. From the letter she learned of her dear friend's passing. The son wrote warmly of Abigail's "constant, ardent, almost sisterly affection" for his mother. Abigail was suffering from a common affliction of the old—watching their friends and family die one by one. Mercy and Abigail's relationship had gone through a series of ups and downs over the decades. In 1805, Mercy published a history of the revolution that painted John in a poor light. After the book was published, a series of heated letters were exchanged between the Adamses and Mrs. Warren, leading to a cooling off of their relationship. It took the intercession of a mutual friend before the three would renew their friendship.

One of the things the politically minded Mrs. Adams enjoyed in her retirement was following and occasionally meddling in the political career of her son, John Quincy. During many of her later years John Quincy and his wife Louisa Catherine were in Europe while he served as the minister to Russia and Great Britain. She followed his career in the papers and through many letters that went back and forth across the Atlantic. Though Abigail would not live long enough to see her son become the sixth president of the United States, she was especially proud of him when he helped negotiate the Treaty of Ghent in 1814 that ended the War of 1812. Just a year before her death she got to experience the joyful return of John Quincy and his family from Europe. Shortly after landing in America, John Quincy and his family traveled to Quincy to see his parents. Abigail recorded the moment her two grandsons, George and John—whom she had helped raise—saw their grandmother: "I ran to the door...The first who sprang out was John, who with his former ardor was around my neck in a moment. George followed half crazy calling out o Grandmother—o Grandmother."

The Will

The winter of 1815-1816 was hard on Abigail as she suffered from cold weather aliments, especially rheumatism. She was very aware of her own mortality and started to think about the world after she was gone. In mid-January 1816, at age 71, Abigail drew up her will. Her years of frugality and her wise investments in government bonds and land had paid off, making the Adamses wealthy in their old age. Her will was unusual in that she left virtually nothing to the men in her life. She began with gifts to her granddaughters of clothing and jewelry; additionally, each received cash payments of between $400 and $750, depending upon their need. The smallest bequests went to Thomas's daughters, both of whom were still children. Additional funds went to her other nieces, her sister-in-law Catherine Smith, a pair of distant cousins, and two female servants. The only two males to receive anything in her will were her two living sons, John Quincy and Thomas. Historians have pondered why she nearly cut out all her male offspring from her will. Possibly she believed the need to provide for the females in her family was very great.

Per the law, her will was meaningless. John could have torn it up with no legal repercussions. In that day, married women had no right to property as their husbands controlled everything. However, John went along with Abigail's wishes and had Thomas disperse the monies and properties as she had requested. Some of the family must have worried about Thomas's ability to carry out his mother's wishes as he was struggling like his younger brother Charles had with alcoholism.

***

In the summer of 1818, before Abigail became ill, President James Monroe stopped by to visit them in their home in Quincy. The Adamses hosted a private dinner party for the president with forty friends. Even though he was a Republican, she viewed his presidency more favorably than Jefferson's or Madison's. Her positive opinion of Monroe was no doubt affected by his choice of John Quincy as the secretary of state.

That fall, Abigail came down with typhoid fever. The disease forced her to bed quickly, where she was nursed by the ladies of the family. The doctors could do little to help, and she died in the early afternoon of Wednesday, October 28. She was buried the next Saturday. Her 83-year-old husband insisted on walking to the meeting house in the funeral procession, though he faltered in the end due to the unseasonable heat. When Thomas Jefferson read in the paper of Abigail's death, he wrote words of condolence to John, for he knew personally of the void that the death of a wife brought: "Tried myself in the school of affliction, by the loss of every form of connection which can rive the human heart, I know well, and feel what you have lost, what you have suffered, are suffering, and have yet to endure." He let John know that "for ills so immeasurable, time and silence are the only medicines."

The End

Thank you for purchasing this book. I hope you enjoyed reading it. Please don't forget to leave a review of the book. I read each one and they help me become a better writer.

-Doug

Timeline of the Life and Times of Abigail Adams

November 22, 1744 (new style calendar) - Born in Weymouth, Massachusetts Bay, British America.

October 25,1764 - Marries John Adams at her parent's home.

1765 - Daughter Abigail "Nabby" is born.

1767 - Son John Quincy is born.

1768 - Daughter Grace Susanna is born, dies as an infant.

1770 - Son Charles is born.

1772 - Son Thomas Boylston is born.

1777 - Daughter Elizabeth is stillborn.

April 1768 - The Adams family moves to Boston.

1774 - The Adams family returns to Braintree due to the unstable political situation in Boston brought about by the impending revolutionary war.

July 1776 - Declaration of Independence is completed. The document declares independence of the American colonies from Great Britain.

September 1783 - The Treaty of Paris is signed, ending the American Revolutionary War.

1784 - Joins John at his diplomatic post in Paris.

1785 - Moves to London to accompany her husband in his role as minister to Britain for the United States.

1788 - The Adams family returns to Massachusetts.

1792 - The city of Quincy is split off from Braintree; the new town is named after Colonel John Quincy, maternal grandfather of Abigail Adams.

March 4,1797 - Becomes the second First Lady of the United States. The Adamses reside in the executive mansion at Philadelphia.

1800 - When the seat of government is moved to Washington, D.C, the First Family moves into the Executive Mansion, or White House as it is now known.

March 4, 1801 - Thomas Jefferson becomes the third president of the United States.

March 4, 1809 - James Madison becomes the fourth president of the United States.

1813 - Daughter Nabby dies of breast cancer.

March 4, 1817 - James Monroe becomes the fifth president of the United States.

October 28, 1818 - Dies at her home of typhoid fever.

March 4, 1825 - John Quincy Adams becomes the sixth president of the United States.

July 4, 1826 - John Adams dies.

Biographical Sketches

Jefferson, Thomas (1743 – 1826) was an American Founding Father who was the principal author of the Declaration of Independence and later served as the third president of the United States. In 1760 he entered the College of William and Mary where he was exposed to the ideas of the Enlightenment and the Age of Reason. After college, he became a lawyer and then a member of the Virginia House of Burgesses. During the Revolutionary period in America, he was a member of the Continental Congress and principal author of the Declaration of Independence. He was an advocate of democracy, republicanism, and individual rights, motivating American colonists to break from Great Britain and form a new nation. Thomas Jefferson served as secretary of state under George Washington then became the second vice president of the United States, serving under John Adams from 1797 to 1801.

Starting in 1801 he became the third president of the United States, with a tone of simplicity and frugality. His first term in office was highlighted by the Louisiana Purchase in 1803, which doubled the size of the United States. His second term was much more contentious, including the British attack on the USS *Chesapeake*; the conspiracy trial of former vice president Aaron Burr; and the Napoleonic Wars in Europe, which diminished commerce between Europe and America. After the presidency, Jefferson retired to his home in Virginia, which he called Monticello, and pursued a wide variety of interests from agriculture to founding the University of Virginia.

Warren, Mercy Otis (1728 – 1814) was an historian, poet, and dramatist during the revolutionary era in America. She was born in Massachusetts into a politically active family. Her brother James made a name for himself in his vocal opposition to the writs of assistance and the Stamp Act. In 1754 Mercy Otis married James Warren with whom she had five children. She was a talented writer, becoming in a manner the poet laureate and later historical apologist for the patriot cause. Through her brother's and husband's connections to revolutionary leaders, she gained access to the inner circle of prominent leaders in the revolution. Her works included several plays and a three-volume history of the revolution published in 1805 titled *History of the Rise, Progress, and Termination of the American Revolution*. In the book, Mercy Otis Warren paints a caustic picture of the leaders who had "aristocratical" ideologies; among these was John Adams.

During the revolutionary period she was a frequent correspondent with John and Abigail Adams and other leading political leaders. After the publication of her history of the revolution she engaged in a lengthy war of words with Mr. Adams over his role in the revolution. He objected to her statements that "his passions and prejudices were sometimes too strong for his sagacity and judgment," that since his sojourn in England he had shown a fondness for monarchy, and that "pride of talents and much ambition, were undoubtedly combined" in his character. The controversy over the book caused a break in the relationship between Mr. and Mrs. Adams and Mrs. Warren that would last for several years. Even though they eventually renewed their friendship, John Adams wrote to Eldridge Gerry that "History is not the Province of the Ladies."

Figure – Portrait of Mercy Otis Warren by John Singleton Copley, circa 1763.

Washington, Martha (1731 – 1802) was the wife of President George Washington. She was born in Kent County, Virginia, to a respected family. In 1749 she married the wealthy planter Daniel Parke Custis. Martha and her husband had four children, two of whom survived into adulthood. Upon the death of her husband in 1757 she inherited a sizable fortune, making her one of the richest widows in Virginia. Two years after the death of her husband, she married a Virginia militia officer named George Washington. The couple moved to George's nearby plantation called Mt. Vernon. Unable to have children of their own, George took on the role of father to her two children, a boy "Jacky" and a girl "Patsy."

When war broke out between the colonials and the British, George became the General in the Continental Army. During the eight long years of the American Revolutionary War, Martha stayed with him at each of the winter camps, tending to his needs and caring for the soldiers. After independence was achieved from Great Britain, General Washington became the first president of the newly formed United States of America. Martha defined the role of what would become known as the First Lady during her husband's two terms as president. As First Lady, she oversaw the social activities in the Executive Mansion that were important to influence the members of Congress. Both George and Martha grieved the death of Patsy in 1773 and Jacky in 1781. When Jacky died, George and Martha took over the upbringing of two of her four children. When General Washington died in 1799, Mrs. Washington went into virtual seclusion in an upper room of at her home at Mt. Vernon until her death three years later.

ABIGAIL ADAMS: FIRST LADY OF THE UNITED STATES

Figure – Portrait of Martha Washington at about age 65.

Note of Quotes

The quotations taken from original letters referenced in the book have had the spelling of some words corrected as well as minor grammatical corrections. Care was taken not to change the original meaning of the letters.

References and Further Reading

Abrams, Jeanne E. *First Ladies of the Republic: Martha Washington, Abigail Adams, Dolley Madison, and the Creation of an Iconic American Role*. New York: New York University Press, 2018.

Boller, Paul F. Jr. *Presidential Wives: An Anecdotal History*. Second Edition. Oxford: Oxford University Press, 1998.

DeGregorio, William A. *The Complete Book of U.S. Presidents, From George Washington to George W. Bush*. New York: Barnes & Noble Publishing, Inc., 2004.

Dictionary of American Biography. New York: Charles Scribner's Sons, 1928-1995.

Holton, Woody. *Abigail Adams*. New York: Free Press, 2009.

McCullough, David. *John Adams*. New York: Simon & Schuster, 2001.

Watson, Robert P. *First Ladies of the United States: A Biographical Dictionary*. Boulder: Lynne Rienner Publishers, Inc., 2001.

West, Doug. *John Adams - A Short Biography*. Missouri: C & D Publications, 2015.

Internet References

Letter dated March 31, 1776, from Abigail Adams to John Adams. Adams Family Correspondence, volume 1. Massachusetts Historical Society. Accessed October 28, 2021. http://www.masshist.org/publications/adams-papers/view?id=AFC01d244

Letter dated April 14, 1776, from John Adams to Abigail Adams. National Archives Founders Online. Accessed October 29, 2021.
https://founders.archives.gov/documents/Adams/04-01-02-0248

Letter dated November 14, 1779, from Abigail Adams to John Adams. National Archives Founders Online. Accessed November 12, 2021.
https://founders.archives.gov/documents/Adams/04-03-02-0174

Acknowledgements

I would like to thank Cynthia West and Lisa Zahn for their help in preparation of this book. All the photographs are from the public domain. The quotes at the beginning of the chapters come from brainyquote.com.

About the Author

Doug West is a retired engineer, small business owner, and experienced non-fiction writer with several books to his credit. His writing interests are general, with expertise in science, history, and biographies. Doug has a B.S. in Physics from the Missouri School of Science and Technology and a Ph.D. in General Engineering from Oklahoma State University. He lives with his wife and little dog "Millie" near Kansas City, Missouri. Additional books by Doug West can be found at https://www.amazon.com/Doug-West/e/B00961PJ8M. Follow the author on Facebook at:
https://www.facebook.com/30minutebooks.

Figure – Doug West (photo by Karina West)

Additional Books in the 30 Minute Book Series

All books are by Doug West unless otherwise noted.

A Short Biography of the Scientist Sir Isaac Newton

A Short Biography of the Astronomer Edwin Hubble

Galileo Galilei – A Short Biography

Benjamin Franklin – A Short Biography

The American Revolutionary War – A Short History

The Astronomer Cecilia Payne-Gaposchkin – A Short Biography

Dr. Walter Reed – A Short Biography by Erin Delong

Coinage of the United States – A Short History

John Adams – A Short Biography

Alexander Hamilton – A Short Biography

The Great Depression – A Short History

Jesse Owens, Adolf Hitler and the 1936 Summer Olympics

Thomas Jefferson – A Short Biography

The French and Indian War – A Short History

The Mathematician John Forbes Nash Jr. – A Short Biography

Vice President Mike Pence – A Short Biography

President Jimmy Carter – A Short Biography

President Ronald Reagan – A Short Biography

President George H. W. Bush – A Short Biography

Dr. Robert H. Goddard – A Brief Biography - Father of American Rocketry and the Space Age

Richard Nixon: A Short Biography - 37th President of the United States

Charles Lindbergh: A Short Biography - Famed Aviator and Environmentalist

Dr. Wernher von Braun: A Short Biography - Pioneer of Rocketry and Space Exploration

Bill Clinton: A Short Biography – 42nd President of the United States

Joe Biden: A Short Biography - 47th Vice President of the United States

Donald Trump: A Short Biography - 45th President of the United States

Nicolaus Copernicus: A Short Biography - The Astronomer Who Moved the Earth

America's Second War of Independence: A Short History of the War of 1812

John Quincy Adams: A Short Biography - Sixth President of the United States

Andrew Jackson: A Short Biography: Seventh President of the United States

Franklin Delano Roosevelt: A Short Biography: Thirty-Second President of the United States

James Clerk Maxwell: A Short Biography: Giant of Nineteenth-Century Physics

Ernest Rutherford: A Short Biography: The Father of Nuclear Physics

Sir William Crookes: A Short Biography: Nineteenth-Century British Chemist and Spiritualist

The Journey of Apollo 11 to the Moon

William Henry Harrison: A Short Biography: Tenth President of the United States

John Tyler: A Short Biography: Eleventh President of the United States

James K. Polk: A Short Biography: Eleventh President of the United States

Samuel Adams: A Short Biography: Architect of the American Revolution

The Mexican-American War: A Short History: America's Fulfillment of Manifest Destiny

History of the Plymouth and Massachusetts Bay Colonies: Pilgrims, Puritans, and the Founding of New England

The History of the Jamestown Colony: America's First Permanent English Settlement

Zachary Taylor: A Short Biography: Twelfth President of the United States

Herbert Hoover: A Short Biography: Thirty-First President of the United States

The Great 1929 Stock Market Crash: A Short History

Christopher Columbus and the Discovery of the Americas

The Formation of the 13 Colonies in America: A Short History

Religion in Colonial America: A Short History

George Washington: A Short Biography: First President of the United States

Dr. Benjamin Rush: A Short Biography: Physician and Founding Father of America

The 1918 Spanish Flu Pandemic in America: A Short History

The Ancient Milesian Philosophers: Thales, Anaximander, Anaximenes: A Short Introduction to Their Lives and Works

Martha Washington: First Lady of the United States: A Short Biography

The First Continental Congress: A Short History

Dwight D. Eisenhower: A Short Biography: 34th President of the United States

The American-British Artist Benjamin West: A Short Biography

Index

Adams, Abigail, 1, 3, 6, 7, 9, 11, 15, 18, 23, 28, 34, 40, 45, 46, 48, 53, 54

Adams, Charles, 3, 4, 17, 19, 38, 39, 43, 45, 53, 58

Adams, John, 5, 7, 9, 10, 18, 23, 28, 30, 45, 46, 47, 48, 49, 53, 54, 57

Adams, John Quincy, 3, 4, 13, 18, 19, 20, 21, 34, 36, 37, 39, 40, 41, 42, 43, 45, 46, 58

Adams, Nabby, 17, 20, 21, 22, 24, 34, 35, 36, 38, 40, 45, 46

Adams, Thomas Boylston, 39, 45

Alien and Sedition Acts, 30

American Revolutionary War, 13, 45, 50, 57

Boston Massacre, 11

Boston Tea Party, 11

Braintree, 8, 17, 22, 23, 25, 37, 45, 46

Burr, Aaron, 30, 47

Continental Army, 13, 17, 50

Cranch, Richard, 7

Declaration of Independence, 16, 17, 18, 32, 45, 47

Democratic-Republican party, 26

Federalist Party, 26, 27

First Continental Congress, 12, 60

Franklin, Benjamin, 18, 19, 57

French and Indian War, 11, 57

Great Britain, 3, 12, 13, 19, 37, 41, 45, 47, 50

Jefferson, Thomas, 19, 20, 24, 26, 30, 32, 43, 46, 47, 57

King George III, iii, 21

Louis XVI, 21

Madison, James, 40, 46

Massachusetts Bay Colony, 6

Monroe, James, 37, 43, 46

Peacefield, 23, 40

Remember the Ladies, 13, 15

Roosevelt, Franklin D., 31

smallpox, 16, 17

Smith, Elizabeth Quincy, 6

Smith, William, 6, 34

Treaty of Ghent, 37, 41

Warren, Mercy Otis, 11, 48, 49

Washington, D.C., 25, 30, 40

Washington, George, 30, 47, 49, 50, 53, 60

Washington, Martha, 9, 24, 29, 32, 51, 53, 60

Made in United States
North Haven, CT
26 May 2024